EASY AS
ABC

S s

**Warren Rylands
and Samantha Nugent**

www.av2books.com

LET'S READ AV² BY WEIGL™
ADDED VALUE • AUDIO VISUAL

Go to **www.av2books.com**, and enter this book's unique code.

BOOK CODE

R 2 6 9 9 4 4

AV² by Weigl brings you media enhanced books that support active learning.

AV² provides enriched content that supplements and complements this book. Weigl's AV² books strive to create inspired learning and engage young minds in a total learning experience.

Your AV² Media Enhanced books come alive with...

Audio
Listen to sections of the book read aloud.

Video
Watch informative video clips.

Embedded Weblinks
Gain additional information for research.

Try This!
Complete activities and hands-on experiments.

Key Words
Study vocabulary, and complete a matching word activity.

Quizzes
Test your knowledge.

Slide Show
View images and captions, and prepare a presentation.

... and much, much more!

Published by AV² by Weigl
350 5ᵗʰ Avenue, 59ᵗʰ Floor
New York, NY 10118

Website: www.av2books.com

Library of Congress Control Number: 2015940622

ISBN 978-1-4896-3541-9 (hardcover)
ISBN 978-1-4896-3543-3 (single user eBook)
ISBN 978-1-4896-3544-0 (multi-user eBook)

Printed in the United States of America in Brainerd, Minnesota
1 2 3 4 5 6 7 8 9 0   19 18 17 16 15

052015
WEP050815

Project Coordinator: Katie Gillespie   Art Director: Terry Paulhus

Weigl acknowledges Getty Images and iStock as the primary image suppliers for this title.

S s

CONTENTS

Let's explore the letter

The uppercase letter **S**

looks like this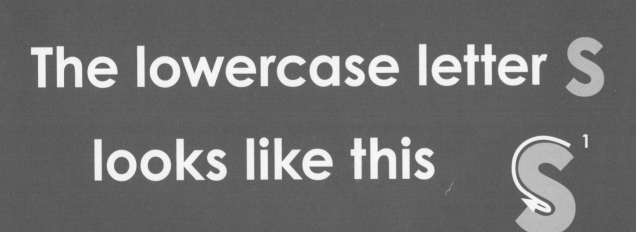

The lowercase letter **s**

looks like this

The letter S can start many words.

Sun

sparrow

sloth

shoes

seahorse

7

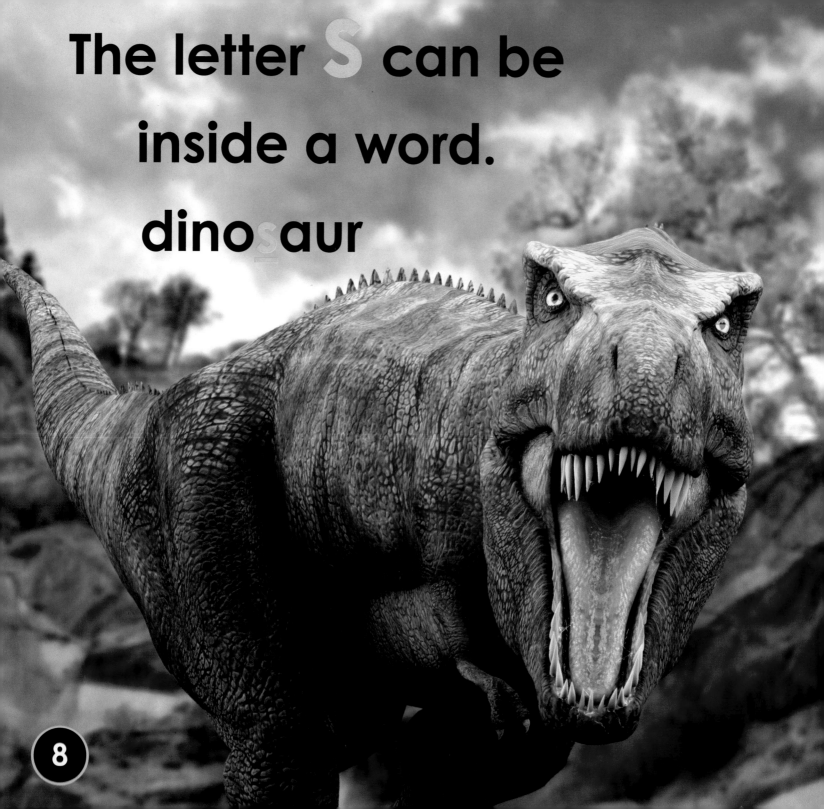

The letter S can be inside a word.

dinosaur

insect

castle

baseball

eraser

9

The letter **S** can be at the end of a word.

player**s**

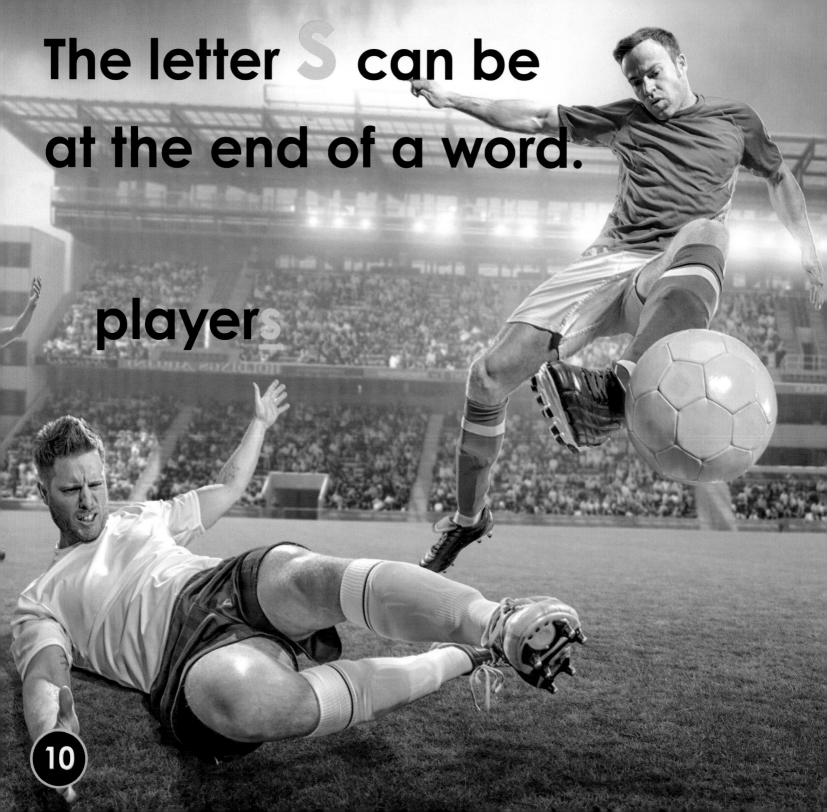

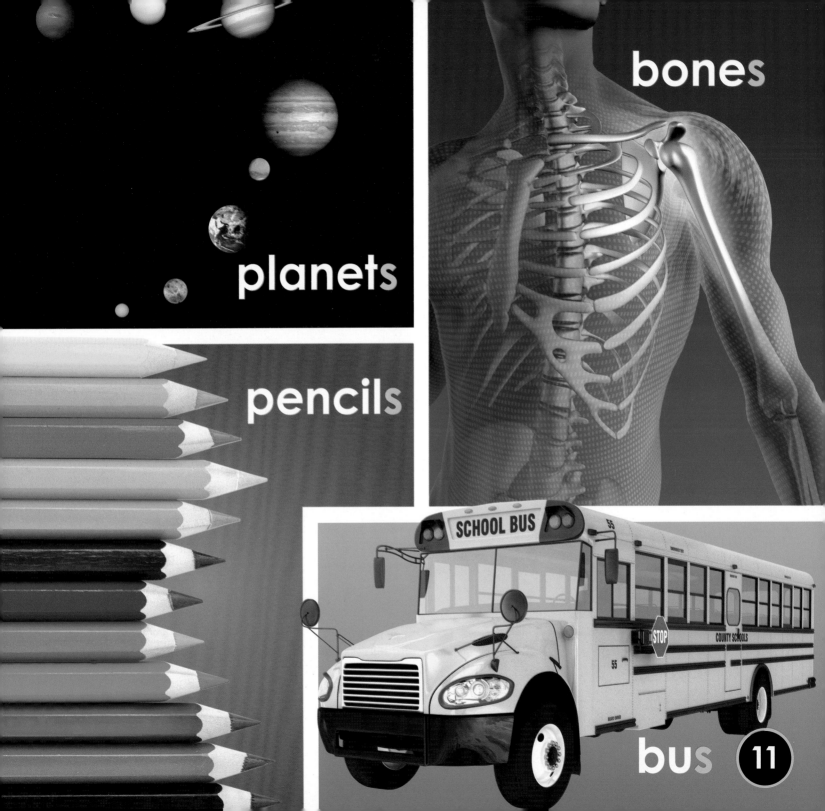

planets

bones

pencils

bus **11**

Many names start with an uppercase S.

Sushant

Sam plays music.

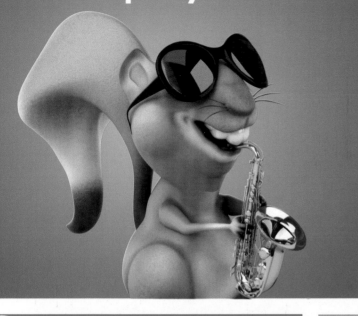

Sandra can surf.

Susan loves to cook.

Shannon likes presents.

13

The letter S makes different sounds.

snake

bells

The letter S  makes the s sound in the word snake.

 The letter S makes the z sound in the word bells.

The letter S makes the s sound in most words.

saw

story

small

first

must

17

In other words, the S makes the z sound.

is

was

close

his

these

19

Having Fun with S

Sheri took the bus
to the baseball game.
The seals were playing
the snails.

Sheri sat next to Steve
on the bus.
Sheri wanted the seals to win.
Steve said the snails
should win.

20

Sheri and Steve stepped
off the bus.
They saw both teams
asleep by first base.

The alphabet
has **26** letters.

S is the nineteenth letter
in the alphabet.

Aa Bb Cc Dd Ee

Ff Gg Hh Ii Jj Kk

Ll Mm Nn Oo Pp

Qq Rr Ss Tt Uu Vv

Ww Xx Yy Zz

23

Ss